Nick Bryant & Rowan Summers

HINKLER BOOKS

Honey Bee

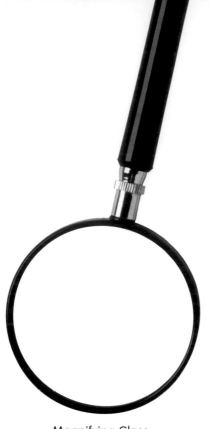
Magnifying Glass

Also available in this series
Spot What Amazing
Spot What Magical
Spot What Spectacular

Sweet Heart

Diving Helmet

Spot What!
First published in 2000 by Hinkler Books Pty. Ltd.
17-23 Redwood Drive, Dingley VIC 3172 Australia
www.hinklerbooks.com

HB
HINKLER
BOOKS

12 14 16 18 20 19 17 15 13 11
08 10 09 07
© Hinkler Books Pty. Ltd. 2000
ISBN:1 8651 5248 X

Dice

Fairy

Printed and bound in China

Dancing Cat

Clarinet

Contents

Globe

Dinosaur

Collected things from many lands,
Are stored within a case.
Can you spot two clowns, a coin,
A sad and happy face,

Two ducks, two dogs, two horses,
Two ways of telling time,
Three locks, five eggs, a pumpkin head
And a red stop sign?

Can you spot an egg of green, a white marshmallow, a gum ball machine,
Two strawberries, a red candy bear, two ice-cream cones, a creamy eclair?
Find two sweet hearts, a car, a muffin, four bananas, and three tiny buttons.

Can you spot a clown
And a pear,
Four jacks, a thimble
And a bear in a chair?

Can you find a
Tomato face,
A horse's head in
A silly place?

There's a rocket ship,
An owl in a tree
And a way to get
From A to B.

spot what

spot
this

SPOT
THAT

9

Can you spot five paper clips
And a Chinese boat,
A rhinoceros, an elephant
And a mountain goat?

Find the stamp from musicland
And a human brain,
A camel and a croissant,
Three different flying planes.

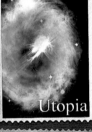

Can you spot a cotton reel,
A nib, a tag and a plug,
A yacht, a dice, a bolt, a key
And a bright red ladybug?

Can you find three house flies,
A needle and a caterpillar,
Two centipedes, two spiders,
A hook, a nail and a gorilla?

Can you spot three arrows,
A window full of clocks,
A tiny little goldfish
And an old mailbox?

Can you find five lemons,
A camera and a cat,
A copy of this page
And a baseball bat?

Can you spot a ship
And a hungry giraffe,
A sign that says FOR SALE,
Three candles in the dark?

ROOM
TO LET

P→

TELEPHONE

LITTER

DR. MORSE'S
Indian Root Pills

GORDON'S
PIANOS

1716

Can you spot a wooden plane,
A piano and a house,
A tractor, trike and windmill,
A little wind up mouse?

Can you find three horses,
A carrot in a truck,
A tamborine, a sewing machine
And a fluffy yellow duck?

16

SPOT WHAT
EXPLORER

Grand Piano

Can you spot a pair
Of scissors,
A wagon wheel and
A shiny mirror,

A pyramid and
A clock,
A dinosaur,
A hose, a sock?

There's a happy ghost,
An old fashioned hat,
A pair of boots
And a dancing cat.

Find a saxophone, a gramophone,
A xylophone, a flute,
Four guitars, three tiny stars,
A golden harp, a lute.

Music makes the world go round,
Seven trumpets can be found,
There's a clarinet, a ukulele too,
They all make wonderful, musical sounds.

☺ The Bank of Smiles

SPOT WHAT

To: Mother Hubbard
Address: The Shoe
NurseryLand

01/01/2000

The more you invest in life, the more you get back from it.

A smile costs nothing, but can mean so much.

Account balance:

1/12/1999

12 laughs   Deposit
17 hugs   Deposit
34 smiles   Deposit
9 tears   Withdrawal

22

Lower Upper Overshot Highway
Station Street
Western Street
market
Forth
Wilce

HAPPY BIRTHDAY

In cert
being
doing
desti
all,
bre
quick
and
sto
loo
p

WITH
MY L

y most beloved,

How happy I was to ...... received your last letter.
......vellous to read all a.........
......nds very exciting. I.........
......een raining here alm.........
......arden, but it does m.........
I've heard that others are going to follow your ...to
Mr. Butcher, Mr. Baker and the local Ca...
all set off to sea in a tub no less. ......on't kn
worthiness of such items but I'm ...re that i
I'm sure you will be joining ...s as so
......you very much and want
......nearts.
All more lo
Duan-Yin.

NOTE

Shopping List:
4 x Bones for the dog.
2 x tins of dog food
1 x bottle of milk
1 Packet of dog biscuits
1 Bottle of dog shampoo
Flea Powder
hair brush

9th

Can you spot a spider,
A medal and a boat,
A telephone, a turtle
And a little love note?

Can you find a bicycle,
A violin and feather,
A map, three green tacks
And five kittens all together?

23

SPOT WHAT

STOP

SPOT WHAT

Can you spot
A bus and a train,
A monkey wrench
And a jet plane?

Six strawberries,
Find them all,
A pair of lips
And a ping pong ball.

Can you find
A big toolbox,
A Christmas hat and
Two Christmas socks?

Can you spot a fisherman,
A peacock and a cat,
A racing horse, a picnic,
A dartboard and a rat?

Can you find the television,
A tower and a gnome,
A little yellow window
And HOME SWEET HOME?

Can you spot a vintage car,
A rabbit and a dog,
A cow, a leaping dolphin
And a little green frog?

Strawberry

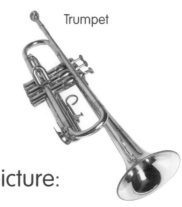
Trumpet

See if you can spot these things in every picture:

Can you find the words SPOT WHAT, A fairy, and a three, A matchstick, an apple, And a honey bee?

Jack

Ball

Rocket Ship

Rules For The Spot What Game

1. Flip a coin to see who goes first.
2. The winner of the coin toss becomes the "caller". The "caller" chooses a picture from the book and picks something for the other person to find saying for example: "Can you Spot a knight in armor?".
3. The "spotter" must then find the item.
4. If the "spotter" can't spot it, the "caller" gets 5 points and shows her where it is. Then,the "caller" takes another turn to choose an item for the "spotter" to spot.
5. If the "spotter" can find the item,then she gets 5 points and it's her turn.
6. The first to reach 30 points wins, but you could also set your own limit of 50 or even 100 points!

You can make the game more challenging by putting a time limit of one to three minutes on each search. Hurry up and start spotting!

Chess Piece

Keys

The Spot What Challenge.

The following items are much harder to find so get ready for the challenge.

Case
(page 4/5)

Wooden Plane

2 owls
A musical note
A lizard
Two knights in armor
The Thinker
A viking ship

Maze
(page 8/9)

A rainbow
4 barrels
The words, "SPOT THIS"
The words, "SPOT THAT"
A man with binoculars
3 horned helmets

Creamy Eclair

Binoculars

Yum
(page 6/7)

A bite
5 bears in a row
2 red twists
The word, "HONEY"
2 lollipops
9 ballons

Stamps
(page 10/11)

2 leopards
2 stamps from nowhere
3 kings
A tiger
A lion
A stamp worth 4 peanuts

Wagon

Wagon Wheel

Gramophone

Bugs
(page 12/13)

Butterfly A
Butterfly B
Butterfly C
A knight in armor
A pig
4 clown faces

Toys
(page 16/17)

Two dinosaurs
An eggbeater
Hammer & wrench
A lion
A purse
The cow that jumped over the moon

Street
(page 14/15)

3 shoes
6 ducks
A lantern
A scary smile
A bonsai garden
A mirror

The Thinker

House
(page 18/19)

7 keys
A fire truck
A skull
A radio
Three chess pieces
The numbers: 1, 2, and 4

Ukulele

Old Radio

Pyramid

Music

(page 20/21)

A banjo
An accordian
A pair of maracas
A bell
A tin whistle
Bongo drums

Red

(page 24/25)

A tractor
Boltcutters
A hardhat
A feather
A clamp
2 boxing gloves

Lute

Corkboard

(page 22/23)

9 brass tacks
"HAPPY BIRTHDAY"
Tic-Tac-Toe
A piano player
A butterfly
A helicopter

Gallery

(page 26/27)

2 carousel horses
A gold teapot
A fork
A wrench
The letters, "OFLCTB"
The words, "THE END"

Toy Soldier

Mouse

Thimble

Chinese Boat

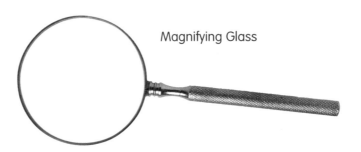
Magnifying Glass

Acknowledgements

We would like to thank the following people:

Albert Meli from Continuous Recall

Sam Grimmer

Peter Tovey Studios

Andrew Curtain

Kate Bryant

Tommy Z

Gillian Banham

Allison McDonald

Rocking Horse

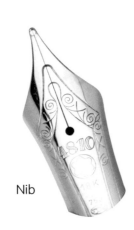
Nib